Origami Butterflies

Book One

Michael G. LaFosse
Richard L. Alexander
and
Greg Mudarri

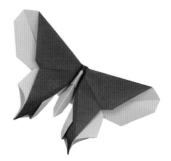

TUTTLE Publishing

Tokyo | Rutland, Vermont | Singapore

Diagram Key

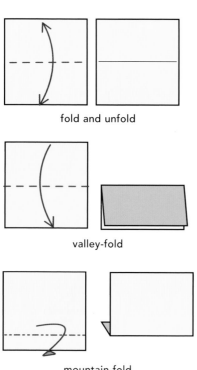

fold and unfold

valley-fold

mountain-fold

fold to indicated line

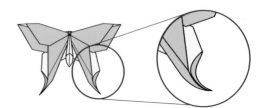

magnification of model

turn model over

rotate model

apply pressure in
direction shown:
squash fold, inside-
reverse fold, etc.

pull-out paper

Contents

The Butterfly Design System

Projects

Using the Butterfly Design System

Discover your own "species" with LaFosse's design system.

Michael LaFosse's origami butterfly design system is based on sequentially squashing rectangular proportions, so there are many possible ways to handle the extra paper available when starting from a square. Some can be temporarily stored in the wingtips, then pulled out to form beautiful color-change patterns. Some can be used to produce a segmented abdomen. Some can be rolled beneath the forewings to accentuate the separation of fore and hindwings. The

LaFosse Moth begins with a blintz to provide even more extra paper for later use in exotic treatments. There are an unlimited number of choices that can be combined in different ways throughout the process of folding the rest of the model.

Have fun by experimenting with the variables of this system and open your mind and hands to the endless possibilities of paper folding.

Butterfly Base Stages

The form will be determined by the choices you make in the following pages.

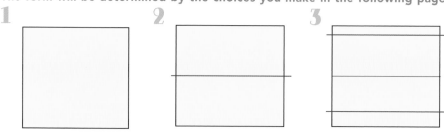

1   2   3

Establish Horizon Line   Margins (pages 6-11)

4

Color Change (page 14)

5

6

7

Squash-folding (page 12)

8

Abdominal/Head
Delineation Fold

9

10

Squash-folding (page 13)

11

90°

Wing Details (page 16)

12

Head Details (pages 17 and 18)

13

Abdominal Taper (page 19)

14

The Butterfly Base

Upper & Lower Margins
(Flaps & Corners)

Astounding variation is derived from just the initial folds. Typically, you fold the paper in half first. This "horizon" fold becomes the butterfly's "waistline" and a portion of the length of the abdomen.

Subsequent margins, from folds made parallel, and toward the horizon (whether forward or backward) are "introductory flaps" which provide diversity.

There are many ways to form margins. The edges could meet the horizon, be folded in at any fraction, or be placed either on the front or folded to the back. It is often easiest to tuck in all or at least some of the corners.

Corner treatments could be either mountain or valley-folds, and there is no reason to be limited to 45 degree angles.

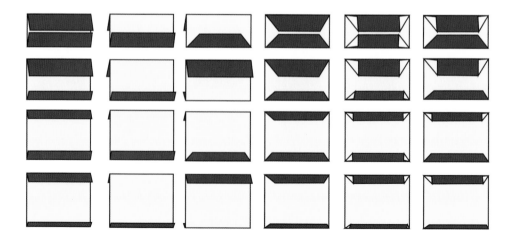

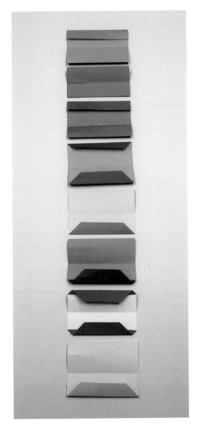 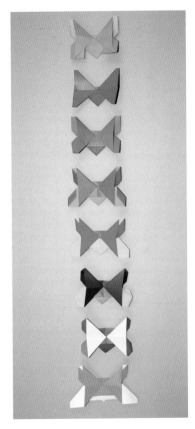

These early steps determine many possible outcomes! Observe the initial
set-up decisions (left), and the resulting bases (right).

Introductory Folds

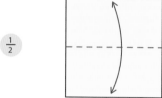

$\frac{1}{2}$

The first fold will almost always be a "book fold." Fold the paper in half with the opposite edges touching, just as you would close a book. This forms the horizon, or waistline, of the butterfly. (When you begin to design your own butterflies, explore what happens when you fold the paper not exactly in half.)

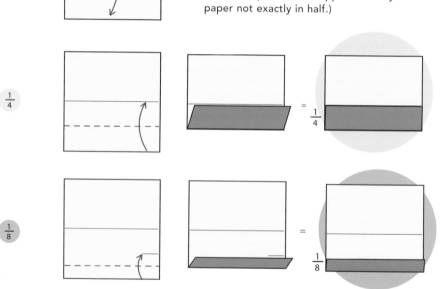

$\frac{1}{4}$

$= \frac{1}{4}$

$\frac{1}{8}$

$= \frac{1}{8}$

When trying to obtain a fold where you only need a reference point to find the correct measurement, make a "pinch" mark at the edge (or edges), instead of a full crease. Shorter fold-overs often require marking both sides for accurate symmetry.

The Origamido Butterfly (left) starts from a double, 1/4 valley-fold (cupboard fold). "The Lillian" (right) starts from 1/8 and 3/16 valley-folds with beveled edges.

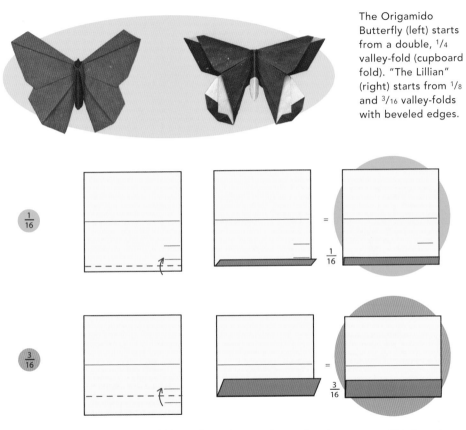

For a 3/16 fold, bring the 1/4 and 1/8 pinch marks together and make a crease. This is perhaps the most popular ratio used in Michael's designs, since it results in a pleasing amount of "top paper" for the wings.

Unless otherwise noted, the corners will be valley-folded to the crease, creating 45-degree angle bevels (you may wish to experiment with other angles).

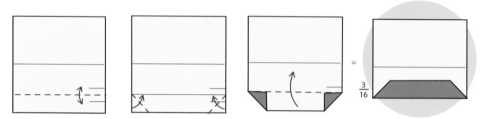

Mountain-folds are shown with dotted lines:

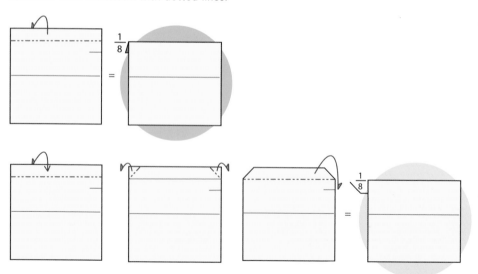

When you experiment, try some initial folds based on proportions other than one half.

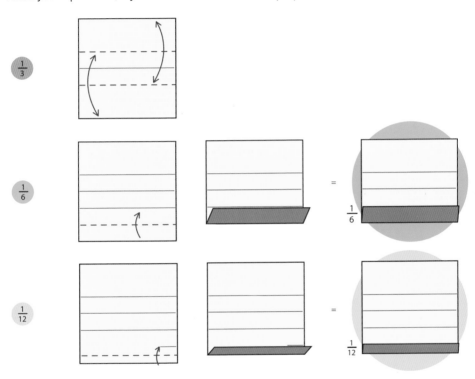

Squash-folding

Technique shown with plain 8.5 x 11" paper, but any rectanglar sheet will do.

This series of squash folds is used in a majority of Michael LaFosse's designs within his butterfly system, so take the time to master and memorize this series of folds carefully.

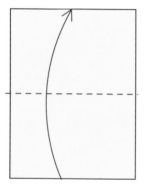

1 Valley-fold in half.

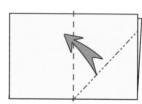

2 Valley-fold in half once again, then stand this half up, perpendicular to the table.

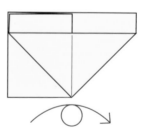

4 Turn over.

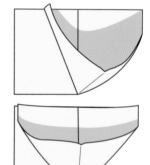

3 Squash-fold, using the existing crease line (second valley fold) to center the squash. (Note: This second line may not always divide the paper exactly in half.)

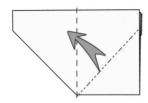

Align the lower right corner to the center of the top. Push the mountain fold flat, directly over the crease line made in the second valley fold.

5 Squash the other flap using the same crease to center the resulting triangle, as before.

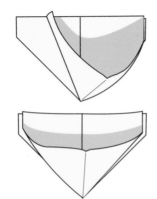

6 Fold corner to end of gap. Arrange corner 90 degrees (perpendicular to the flaps).

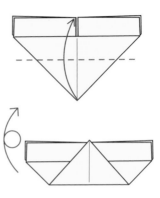

7 Turn over so the triangular corner is flat on the table.

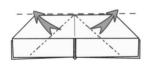

8 Open by squashing both wings using the new crease to center the wing flaps.

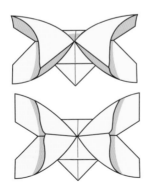

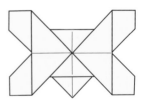

9 Finished base for LaFosse's original 8½ x 11" origami butterfly.

Color Change

The LaFosse origami butterflies typically have two layers showing on the wings: "top paper" and "tip paper." If you choose to fold the paper in half as a valley-fold, the "top paper" will be same color as is on the outside of the folded packet. This system displays color contrasts and patterns beautifully, so take charge of what shows, not only on the wings, but on the head and abdomen! This decision allows the flaps to be manipulated for pattern and design (as shown in our next variable, wing details).

Below is only one example showing the effects of this single decision. (Remember that your previous choices also affect the outcome.)

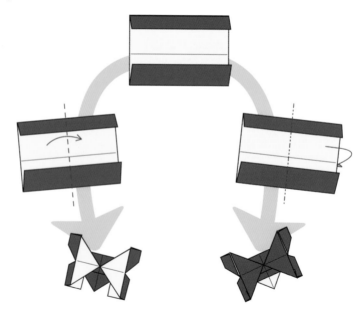

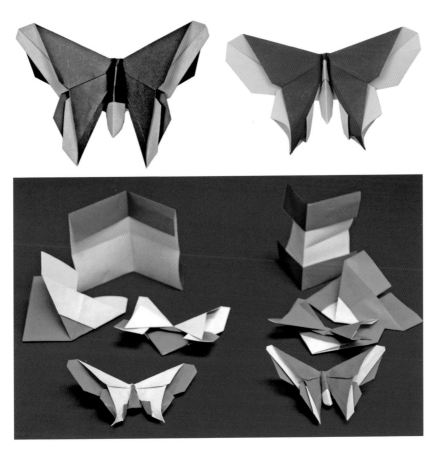

The decision in this step is partly demonstrated in the differences between "The Nolan" (left) and "The Baxter" (right), for example.

Wonderful Wings

Wing patterns and details make the butterfly. You may discover dozens of possibilities as you explore the landscape of a square sheet of paper. Apply your designs to many different types and sizes of papers for an infinite variety of new species.

The examples to the right illustrate a few wing variants using the Origamido Butterfly.

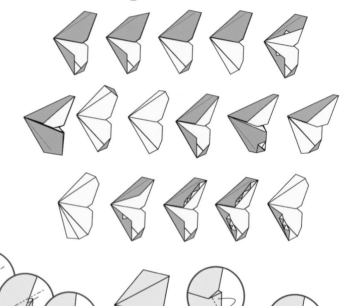

When you separate the forewings from the hind-wings with a crimp, accentuate the separation with an inside reverse-fold. This resulting notch allows additional wing separation and wing detail possibilities using the newly formed layers. Since it is quite small, the wing notch fold is shown up-close, in detail. After the notch is made, further indentation is possible, as shown in the right-most two circles above.

Butterfly Head Style 1

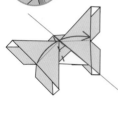

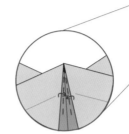

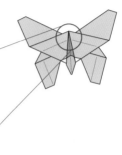

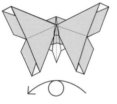

1 Form body between the two wings, creating a point at the top. Turn over.

2 Make a slight pinch on the underside, bringing mountain-folded edges to the center, just in the head area. Turn over.

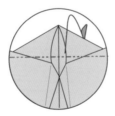

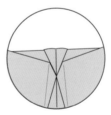

3 Press center mountain to squash the head area flat. Two smaller mountain folds result.

4 Fold flattened point to the underside.

5 The Style #1 head.

Butterfly Head Style 2

Use the following head when the top of the body does not come to a sharp, single point.

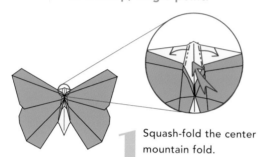

1 Squash-fold the center mountain fold.

2 Inside reverse-fold the new corners into the center.

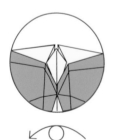

3 Turn over.

4 Valley-fold new flaps below where they will not show.

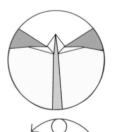

5 Turn over.

6 The Style #2 head.

Abdominal Taper

Before

After

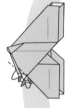

Close the wings together and fold the excess bottom corners inside the body. Note in the detail that you must pinch the layers together and fold the corners in. You do not have to open the body paper too much to do this. After the corners have been tucked in, notice that the taper of this fold narrows towards the back end of the butterfly's body.

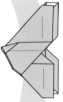

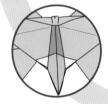

A Butterfly for Alice Gray

As a teen, Michael met with Alice Gray, an eminent entomologist from the American Museum of Natural History (and an origami advocate). While they conversed, Michael nervously folded paper. Lo and behold, a new origami butterfly was born! Michael perfected the model, and named it for Alice.

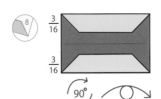

1 Start with a 3/16 beveled introductory fold on both sides. Rotate and turn over the model.

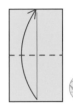

2 Valley-fold in half. Begin procedure for squash-folding.

3 Final wing squashes.

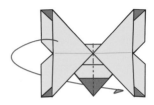

4 Mountain-fold in half.

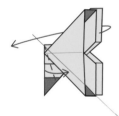

5 Fold body over top wing paper (use the superimposed line as a guide), allowing the wing paper to come out below.

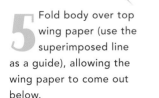

6 Fold wing to wing, sandwiching body paper between.

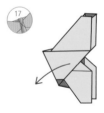

7 Refer to page 17 to create the head using butterfly head fold #1. Use the abdominal taper as shown on page 19.

The Lillian

This butterfly is named for Lillian Oppenheimer, founder of the Origami Center of America, for doing so much to popularize origami. Lillian's dream for people to share friendship through origami has been continued and expanded by OrigamiUSA.

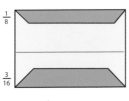

1 Start with a 3/16 beveled introductory fold on the bottom and a 1/8 bevel on the top. Rotate and turn over.

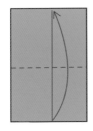

2 Begin squash-folding.

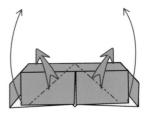

3 Wing Squashes.

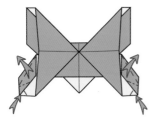

4 Base. Swivel-fold hindwings to form shape in diagram #5.

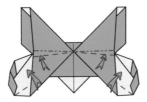

5 Roll the bottom edge of each hind-wing as far as it can go (while remaining flat to the bottom corner). Crimp (mountain and valley-fold at the mid-section of the wings) to flatten paper and form wing separation.

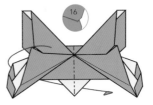

6 Apply wing-notch technique. Mountain-fold in half.

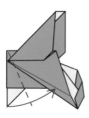

7 Fold body paper over the top wing paper, allowing other wing's paper to come out from beneath.

8 Fold wing to wing, sandwiching the body between. Apply butterfly head fold #1.

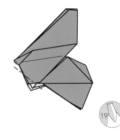

9 Apply abdominal taper.

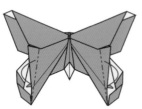

10 Open. Mountain-fold shown edges inside.

The Lillian Butterfly in various colors and treatments folded from handmade duo papers produced at Origamido Studio.

Evangeline Fritillary

Evangeline (Van) Rossi encouraged Michael to pursue his artistic interests while he spent time with the Rossi family at their summer camp as a youth. The beautiful natural surroundings also inspired her son, Paul, to become a painter.

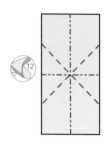

1 Fold a 2 x 1 rectangle in half both ways. Perform the usual squash for the result in Step 2.

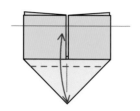

2 Fold bottom corner up center, but not to the top.

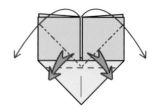

3 Squash wings.

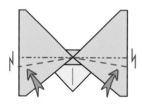

4 Crimp (roll hindwings under the forewing.

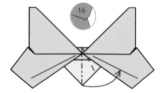

5 The result. Apply wing-notch details. Fold abdomen point over to touch mountain.

6 Fold the wing together, sandwiching the body.

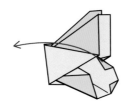

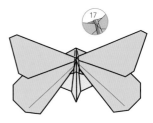

7 Fold the wing-notch corners down. Round the hindwing corners with valley-folds.

8 Open wings.

9 Apply head style #1.

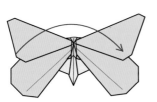

10 Close the wings.

11 Apply Abdominal taper. Open wings.

Alexander Aztec Swallowtail

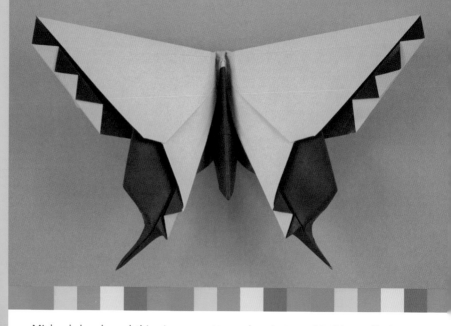

Michael developed this zig-zag patterned variation with "Aztec-like" triangular decorations. The model helps to illustrate how the excess paper can be used to full visual advantage.

1 As before, start with a 3/16 beveled introductory fold on the lower front, and a 1/8 bevel on the back of the top. Make sure the 3/16 bevel is an outer bevel, showing corners on the front. (That is the only difference at the start of this model from the Alexander Swallowtail.) Rotate and turn over.

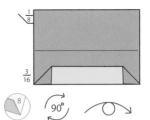

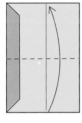

2 Begin squash-folding.

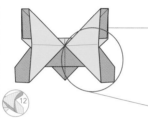

3 Valley-fold from the center of the horizon, to the lower corner of the hindwing. Fold the new area in half to make the image in step 4.

4 Keep new corner intact. Pull the paper folded beneath. This creates excess paper that will not lie flat.

5 Keep the new corner in place. and the paper flat while you "fan-fold" back and forth to create the pattern in step 6.

6 Fold both hindwings to this stage.

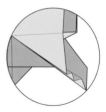

7 Pull hidden forewing tip paper out as far as possible. Crease to flatten (See step 8).

8 Crimp (roll mountain-fold on the inner edge of the forewing downward, creating a valley-fold). This creates a new corner at top.

9 Fold outer-corner over, aligning the edge with mountain crease from the previous step.

10 Valley-fold paper back from where the colors meet. Bring the triangle-tip back to the same point.

 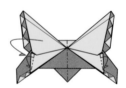 

11 Apply wing-notch technique. Repeat with other wing.

12 Mountain-fold the paper under the wing-notch. Fold model in half.

13 Mountain-fold the body over the hindwing, aligning tip of abdomen to meet the bottom edge of the hindwing. Allow the other wing to come with it.

14 Fold other wing over, sandwiching body. Open, apply butterfly head fold #1.

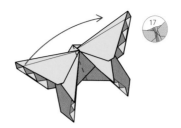

15 Apply abdominal taper.

16 Hindwing detail. Mountain-fold behind.

17 Inside-reverse.

18 Pinch a mountain-fold, and curl each swallowtail point.

curl

19 Result.

Published by Tuttle Publishing, an imprint of Periplus Editions (HK) Ltd.

www.tuttlepublishing.com

Library of Congress Cataloging-in-Publication Data

LaFosse, Michael G.
  Origami butterflies / Michael G. LaFosse. -- 1st ed.
    p. cm.
  Includes bibliographical references and index.
  ISBN 978-0-8048-4027-9 (kit : alk. paper)
1. Origami. 2. Butterflies in art. I. Title.
  TT870.L23428 2009
  736'.982--dc22

                          2008036920

ISBN 978-0-8048-4027-9

DISTRIBUTED BY

North America, Latin America & Europe
Tuttle Publishing
364 Innovation Drive
North Clarendon, VT 05759-9436
U.S.A.
Tel: 1 (802) 773-8930
Fax: 1 (802) 773-6993
info@tuttlepublishing.com
www.tuttlepublishing.com

Asia Pacific
Berkeley Books Pte. Ltd.
61 Tai Seng Avenue #02-12
Singapore 534167
Tel: (65) 6280-1330
Fax: (65) 6280-6290
inquiries@periplus.com.sg
www.periplus.com

First edition
15 14 13 12 11   1105EP
9 8 7 6 5 4
Printed in Hong Kong

Diagrams by Michael G. LaFosse
Illustration by Greg Mudarri
Photography by Michael G. LaFosse, Richard Alexander, and Greg Mudarri

Video instructions for folding these projects, and many others, are available on DVD from Origamido Studio, www.origamido.com.

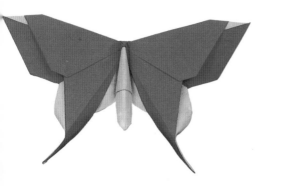

Origami Butterflies

Book Two

Michael G. LaFosse
Richard L. Alexander
and
Greg Mudarri

TUTTLE Publishing

Tokyo | Rutland, Vermont | Singapore

Diagram Key

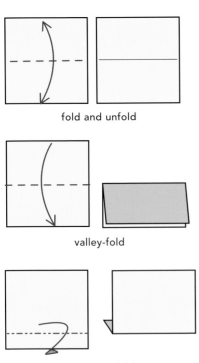

fold and unfold

valley-fold

mountain-fold

fold to indicated line

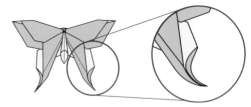

magnification of model

turn model over

rotate model

apply pressure in
direction shown:
squash fold, inside-
reverse fold, etc.

pull-out paper

Contents

Projects (Cont'd)

Alexander Swallowtail

Perhaps Michael's most popular swallowtail design, Michael named this butterfly for Richard L. Alexander, co-founder of Origamido Studio. Michael has developed many swallowtail butterfly designs using the curling technique familiar to people who have folded the traditional iris or lily.

1. Start with a 3/16 beveled introductory fold on the bottom and a 1/8 bevel behind the top. Rotate and turn over.

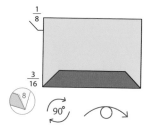

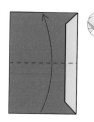

2. Valley-fold in half, beginning the squash-folding procedure.

3. The base figure. Roll each top hindwing inner edge over as far as it can go, flat, to each bottom corner. Crimp (mountain and valley-fold at the midsection of the wings) to flatten the paper and form wing separations.

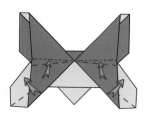

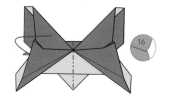

4. Apply wing-notch technique. Mountain-fold model in half.

5. Fold body over the top paper of the hindwing, allowing other wing to come out from beneath.

6. Fold wing to wing, sandwiching the body between. Apply butterfly head fold #1.

7 Apply abdominal taper.

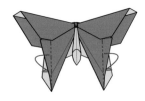

8 Open. Mountain-fold shown edges inside.

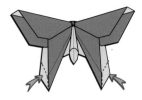

9 Form each "swallowtail" by pinching a mountain fold at the bottom corner, following upward to the crease along each inner folded edge. Push inward.

10 Mountain-fold shown edge behind to narrow the point. Pinch and curl outward to make a graceful shape.

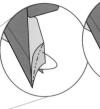

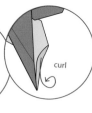

curl

11 Result.

12 Fold top edges of forewing tips back, allowing a small triangle of color to show. (This is optional, and you could also try folding the shape in front, hiding the color spot.)

The Baxter

Michael named this model for Jonathan Baxter, an enthusiastic folder born in New Zealand. For several years he worked tirelessly to put Charlotte, North Carolina, on the origami map with his Southeastern Origami Festivals.

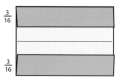

1 Start with a ³⁄₁₆ introductory fold on the front top and bottom. Rotate.

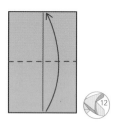

2 Begin squash-folding.

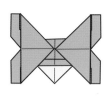

3 Result.

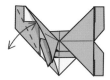

4 Open wing and pull out free paper from top area as far as it will go while staying flat. Put the paper back inside the wing.

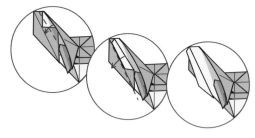

5 Fold indicated edge to crease. Fold multi-layered shape over, using crease as hinge. Close top layer of wing. Repeat steps 4 & 5 with other wing.

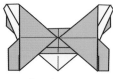

6 Result.

7 Open top layer of the hindwings and pull out the free paper from inside the bottom area as far as it can go while staying flat.

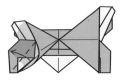

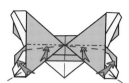

8 Roll top layer of hindwing upward, stopping at the hind corner. Crimp (mountain and valley-fold at the mid-section of the wings) to flatten.

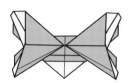

9 Apply wing-notch technique. See diagram #10.

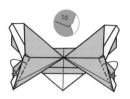

10 Mountain-fold indicated edges behind.

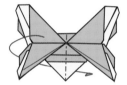

11 Mountain-fold in half, wing to wing.

12 Fold body paper over the top hindwing, allowing other wing to come from beneath. Match corner point of abdomen to crease on hindwing. Fold intersects top center of head.

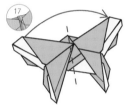

13 Fold wing to wing, sandwiching body between. Open. Apply head style #1.

14 Apply abdominal taper. Open the wings.

The Michael Shall

LaFosse named this butterfly for Michael Shall, an origami enthusiast from New York City. Michael Shall, Lillian Oppenheimer and Alice Gray transformed a New York-based group of folders into a not-for-profit organization to promote the sharing of origami; OrigamiUSA is their legacy.

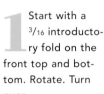

1 Start with a ³/₁₆ introductory fold on the front top and bottom. Rotate. Turn over.

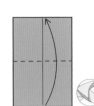

2 Begin squash-folding.

3 Result.

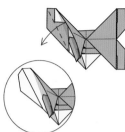

4 Open wing and pull out free paper from top area as far as it will go while staying flat. Repeat on other wing.

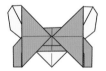

5 Result.

6 Open top paper of the hindwings and pull out free paper from inside the bottom area as far as it can go while staying flat.

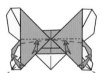

7 Roll top paper of the hindwings upward, stopping at hind corners. Crimp (mountain and valley-fold at the midsection of the wings) to flatten.

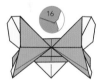

8 Your paper will look like this. Apply wing-notch technique.

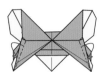

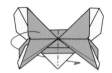

9 Mountain-fold indicated edges behind.

10 Mountain-fold in half, wing-to-wing.

11 Fold the body paper over the top wing paper, allowing the wing paper to come out from underneath. Make the corner point of the body touch the crease on the hindwing. The fold made should travel to the top corner of the head paper.

12 Fold wing to wing, sandwiching body between. Open. Apply head style #1.

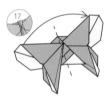

13 Use the abdominal taper. Open the wings.

14 Bring out the hidden corners from inside the hindwings.

15 Fold corners in to form patterns on each hindwing. Curl the tips of the hindwings (optional).

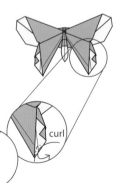

curl

The Temko

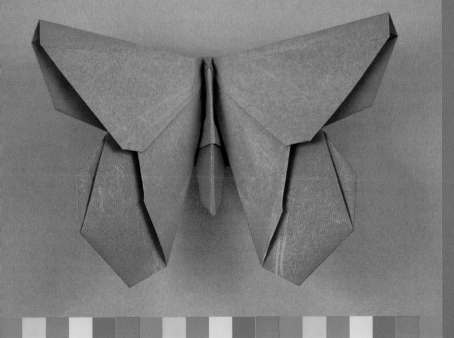

Michael named this butterfly for Florence Temko, an authority on paper-folding and paper arts, and author of dozens of origami publications from England and America. Florence was one of the most prolific authors of origami books that Michael devoured as a youngster.

1 Make a 3/16 introductory fold on the front bottom, and a 1/8 bevel on the behind the top. Unfold bottom front layer.

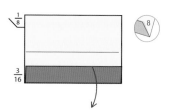

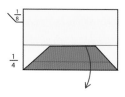

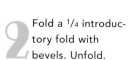

2 Fold a 1/4 introductory fold with bevels. Unfold.

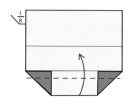

3 Re-fold bottom edge using the 3/16 crease from step #1.

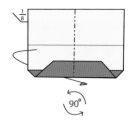

4 Mountain-fold in half, short edge to short edge. Rotate.

5 Squash.

6 Turn over.

7 Squash.

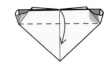

8 Pull out layer from wider side.

9 Fold in front.

10 Squash sides flat, aligning bottom corners of top layer shape with crease below.

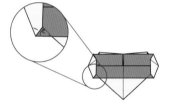

11 Close-up: Fold bottom edge to crease. Repeat with other wing.

12 Fold top down to the point.

13 Squash.

14 Roll top layer of forewing downward, matching top corner to folded edge below. Crimp (mountain and valley-fold at the mid-section of the wings) to flatten. Apply wing-notch technique.

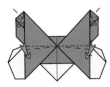

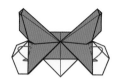

15 Fold corners inside.

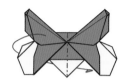

16 Mountain-fold, wing to wing.

17 Fold the body paper over top paper of hindwing, allowing other wing out from beneath. Align abdomen point to crease on hindwing. Fold to the top center of head.

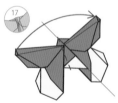

18 Fold wings together. Apply head style #1.

19 Apply abdominal taper. Open the wings.

Origamido
Butterfly

Michael named this butterfly for the Origamido Studio, a special place founded by Richard L. Alexander and he in 1996. In comparison to many of the other models, the Origamido Butterfly uses a different aspect of Michael's system. Consider these methods for your own designs.

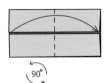

1 Start with two, ¹/₄ introductory folds (cupboard fold).

2 Valley-fold short edges together. Rotate so the folded edge is on the bottom.

3 Squash.

4 Turn over.

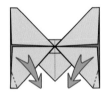

5 Squash.

6 Fold bottom point up along the center gap, making sure to leave a margin at top (not folding it completely in half). Unfold.

7 Keep all of the layers neatly together. Squash.

8 Open top layers of hindwings, squash trapped paper to lie flat.

9 Crimp (mountain-fold along existing horizon, bring outside ends of the mountain fold down). The leading edge of the forewing will change as you do this. Carefully turn hindwing corners inside-out.

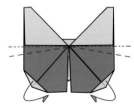

10 Valley-fold forewing papers up, and mountain-fold hindwing corners under.

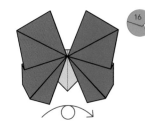

11 Apply wing-notch technique. Turn over.

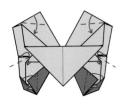

12 Valley-fold raw edges of forewing papers to the indicated folded edges. Valley-fold wing separation corners down. Mountain-fold hindwing papers under.

13 Valley-fold upper layer papers over leading edge and tuck under triangular layers.

14 Valley-fold in half.

15 Fold wings to meet, sandwiching body between. Open.

16 Apply head style #2 (since the center does not come to a sharp point).

The Joyce Rockmore

Michael named this butterfly for Joyce Rockmore, a founder of Paperfolders In New England (PINE), and TV personality of a cable-access show in Brockton, Massachusetts called Everybody Folds Something. Joyce enjoyed sharing new origami projects with friends.

1 Start with three pinch marks, dividing the remainder in $1/2$ each time to find the upper one-eighth, then book fold in half.

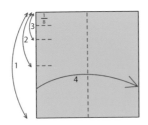

2 Valley-fold lower short edge to $1/8$ pinch mark.

3 Squash.

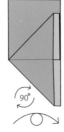

4 Rotate. Turn over.

5 Squash.

6 Fold upper corner to bottom center. Unfold.

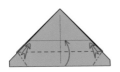

7 Open to mark and squash corners.

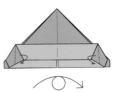

8 Fold tips behind. Turn over.

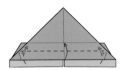

9 Open to mark and squash.

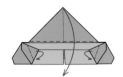

10 Fold tips behind. Fold upper corner down over.

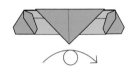

11 Turn over.

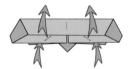

12 Open and squash.

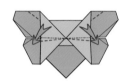

13 Crimp wing separation by swinging forewings downward.

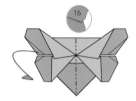

14 Fold in half. Wing-notch detail.

15 Align abdomen tip to superimposed reference, allowing other wing to come out from beneath.

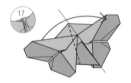

16 Fold other wing over to match tips and notches, sandwiching body between. Apply head style #1.

17 Apply abdominal taper. Open.

The Nolan

Michael named this butterfly for origami artist and author J.C. Nolan. During an origami convention in New York City, Jay approached Michael about diagramming Michael's designs. Jay was on the cutting edge of using computer graphics programs for diagramming origami folds.

1 Start with a 3/16 introductory fold on the bottom front side, and the top back. Rotate.

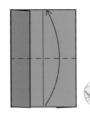

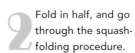

2 Fold in half, and go through the squash-folding procedure.

3 Base result.

4 Open the top paper of each wing and pull out free paper from inside top area as far as it can go, remaining flat.

5 Forewings look like this (wing shown open). Repeat on other wing.

6 Roll top layer of hindwing up, stopping at the hindwing corner. Crimp (mountain and valley-fold at the mid-section of the wings) to flatten.

7 Apply wing-notch technique.

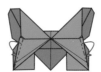

8 Mountain-fold indicated edges behind.

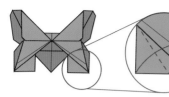

9 Hindwing: Where lower flap emerges, fold corner up to area where colors separate.

10 Fold new corner to indicated area.

11 Unfold.

12 Inside-reverse.

13 Unfold flap.

14 Fold corner to indicated line.

15 Replace original folds with corner hidden inside.

16 Valley-fold and unfold.

17 Inside-reverse fold.

18 The wing will look like this. Repeat on the other side.

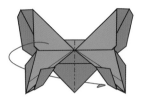

19 Mountain-fold model in half.

20 Fold abdomen tip to the indicated crease line, letting the other wing come from beneath.

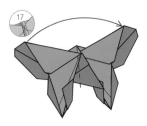

21 Fold wings together, sandwiching the body. Apply head style #1.

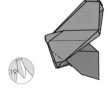

22 Apply abdominal taper.

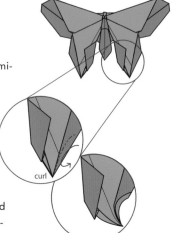

23 Pinch mountain-folds and curl the hindwings slightly.

curl

The LaFosse Moth

This moth's design is quite different from the other projects in this kit, as you will see from the first step of "blintzing" (folding the corners to the center). It still obeys Michael's system of fractional set-up, followed by a sequential series of squash-folds.

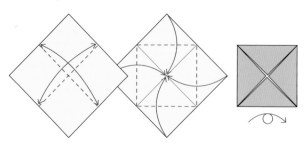

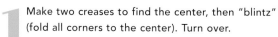

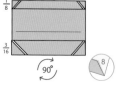

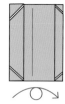

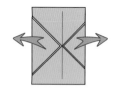

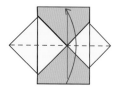

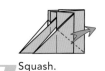

1 Make two creases to find the center, then "blintz" (fold all corners to the center). Turn over.

2 Treat the doubled packet as if it were a single-layer square.

Use a 3/16 introductory fold on the front side bottom and a 1/8 fold on the front top. Rotate.

3 Turn over.

4 Open flaps.

5 Valley-fold in half.

6 Valley-fold the vertical crease.

7 Squash.

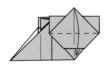

8 Valley-fold triangular flaps down.

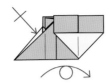

9 Repeat steps 7 and 8 on the opposite side.

10 Fold bottom corner to the top of the central gap and unfold.

11 Squash wings (see step # 12).

12 Pull the paper in the forewings as much as possible and crease flat. Squash the hindwings outward. Pull out top layer at abdomen point.

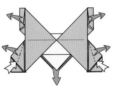

13 The result.

14 An x-ray view: Lift folded edge up and flatten. (Curve this fold to allow it to happen.)

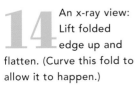

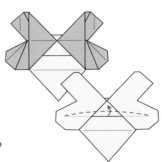

15 Zig-zag this flap. Fold mountains and valleys back- and-forth for the abdomen segments (see step 16).

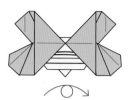

16 The result. Turn over.

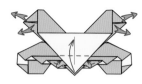

17 Widen the forewings by pulling out paper flattening again. Fold corner of top layer up. Fold lower abdomen corners over.

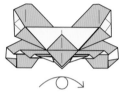

18 The result. Turn over.

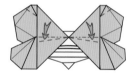

19 Crimp. (Roll the paper over starting from the mountain-crease in the center of the wings. It will pull the top corners of the forewings down. Flatten. Wing-notch details are optional.)

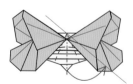

20 Fold in half. Swing abdomen tip to the indicated line, then fold the wings together.

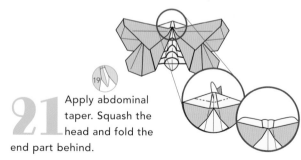

21 Apply abdominal taper. Squash the head and fold the end part behind.

Inspiration

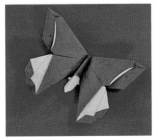

Published by Tuttle Publishing, an imprint of Periplus Editions (HK) Ltd.

www.tuttlepublishing.com

Library of Congress Cataloging-in-Publication Data

LaFosse, Michael G.
  Origami butterflies / Michael G. LaFosse. -- 1st ed.
    p. cm.
  Includes bibliographical references and index.
  ISBN 978-0-8048-4027-9 (kit : alk. paper)
1. Origami. 2. Butterflies in art. I. Title.
  TT870.L23428 2009
  736'.982--dc22
                    2008036920

ISBN 978-0-8048-4027-9

DISTRIBUTED BY

North America, Latin America & Europe
Tuttle Publishing
364 Innovation Drive
North Clarendon, VT 05759-9436
U.S.A.
Tel: 1 (802) 773-8930
Fax: 1 (802) 773-6993
info@tuttlepublishing.com
www.tuttlepublishing.com

Asia Pacific
Berkeley Books Pte. Ltd.
61 Tai Seng Avenue #02-12
Singapore 534167
Tel: (65) 6280-1330
Fax: (65) 6280-6290
inquiries@periplus.com.sg
www.periplus.com

First edition
15 14 13 12 11   1105EP
9 8 7 6 5 4
Printed in Hong Kong

Diagrams by Michael G. LaFosse
Illustration by Greg Mudarri
Photography by Michael G. LaFosse, Richard Alexander, and Greg Mudarri

Video instructions for folding these projects, and many others, are available on DVD from Origamido Studio, www.origamido.com.